The Perspective of the Constellation

The Perspective of the Constellation

Poems

VOLUME 17

Wendy E. Slater

The Perspective of the Constellation
Copyright © 2023 by Wendy E. Slater
traduka.com

All rights reserved. No part of this book may be reproduced in any form or by any means, electronic or mechanical, including photocopying, recording, or by any information storage and retrieval system, without permission in writing from the publisher.

Wendy E. Slater books are available for order through
Ingram Press Catalogues

Published by Traduka Publishing
traduka@traduka.com

Paper ISBN: 978-1-943512-05-8
E-book: 978-1-943512-06-5

BOOK DESIGN BY STREETLIGHT GRAPHICS
AUTHOR PHOTO BY JEFF WOODWARD
COVER PHOTO BY WENDY E. SLATER

For the Truth
And
The Path
To it

Invocation for Peace

TOGETHER let us hold the intention that all aspects of this living planet come together in love, acceptance, and celebration of both our diversities and commonalities. Let us possess the common purpose that we heal from our hearts into compassion and forgiveness for ourselves. Together let us own the belief that we will no longer unite with blame and judgment, but come to accept that we all carry the same wounds. In acknowledging this, the hope is for the whole planet in its jubilant diversity to be healed from any and all woundings so that we come together on equal footing, living in peace and joy and setting the tone for a future of harmony within and on this planet.
Peace to all and healing to all.

CONTENTS

Invocation for Peace vii

1701 Criminally exposed 1

1702 Dimmed in vision 2

1703 Tapped into Truth 3

1704 Love disguised 4

1705 Blended unconsciousness 5

1706 there is the decaying 6

1707 The sun 7

1708 To rekindle 8

1709 What 10

1710 6 days into space 11

1711 The longest dark night 12

1712 To surrender requires 14

1713 The Big Bang 16

1714 If the Dance Is in the Heart 17

1715 An angle is such 21

1716	I need to know	22
1717	What's in the graced	23
1718	Do you know	28
1719	And in the voice	30
1720	What is the sign	32
1721	Division into division	33
1722	Beech leaves	34
1723	Division into dawn	35
1724	Color-coded	36
1725	Objectification is	37
1726	In the calm of it all	38
1727	Historic trauma	39
1728	A never expired star	41
1729	The energy field of trust	42
1730	In that fire	43
1731	Like the accordion	44
1732	Faces strung out	45
1733	Shadow	46
1734	It's like being set up	47
1735	Isolated and separated	48
1736	A rendering to the bone	49

1737	Is this all playing out as	50
1738	Perhaps	51
1739	Everyone's here	52
1740	Grief	53
1741	The anxiety	54
1742	If the heart	55
1743	The surrender	56
1744	If the painted sky	57
1745	The difference lies	58
1746	What is freedom	59
1747	If the constellation	60
1748	The trajectory was way	61
1749	If there was a chain	62
1750	An isolated echo	63
1751	That tired	64
1752	Speaking truth	65
1753	Not being seen in truth	66
1754	Textures and scents	67
1755	The truth of injustice	68
1756	Burrowed and alive	69
1757	The collective	70

1758	Paranoia	71
1759	Flashing sporadic	72
1760	To be found, discovered	73
1761	Folded into an alone	74
1762	Forever alone	75
1763	I wonder where	76
1764	Why is there such	77
1765	All cycles run their	78
1766	Long	79
1767	I am never going	80
1768	Rambling voices	81
1769	Dedication to self	82
1770	Using	83
1771	Visible tears	84
1772	Beautiful hair	85
1773	Safety lies	86
1774	Perhaps	87
1775	Translucent depth	88
1776	Exposed shoulder	89
1777	Trespass in plain sight	90
1778	Stillness	91

1779	Back against a board	92
1780	The sacred truth	93
1781	To feel obligated	94
1782	I am so struck	95
1783	Patience runs too deep	96
1784	The gloved, wonder of	97
1785	The love of it all	98
1786	Used goods	99
1787	Why is this beauty	100
1788	Territoriality	101
1789	Bubbles in a puddle	102
1790	Is this winding path	103
1791	Resilience	104
1792	I am so done	105
1793	What does it feel like	106
1794	What's it like to miss me	107
1795	What is the mystery	108
1796	I shifted	109
1797	Truth of navigation	110
1798	The fallacy	111
1799	Truth in navigation	112

17100 Resiliency 113

17101 Finally uncovering 114

17102 Beyond the looted 115

17103 It is strangely challenging 116

17104 Fertile land 117

17105 Circumnavigating 118

The Perspective of the Constellation

1701

Criminally exposed
    Like a stalker
Streaking through
    Constellations
Robbing
    1 star,
      2 and 3
    All
Folding into
The Mask
    Like the
      Impersonator
        Pretending to hold
          In gangly
            Arms
              The truth.

1702

Dimmed in vision,
    The angle
Held at bay
    By the idea,
Obstructions held too
      Close to the eye and heart
      Hold the illusion.

A lack of
    Comprehensive overview
        In
Horizon, depth, and vibrancy
      And so far
    It holds no sense of
        Urgency nor
           Constructed agenda.

1703

Tapped into Truth
    Discrete intervals
    Determined moments
Cause the fluid stream
      Of thought
   To be veiled
   So close to the light
    But bound to
     Your darkness.

1704

Love disguised
    As a thief
Is no longer
    Bound to the shadow's eclipse
    As apparently
The outline is distinctively
    Apart.

1705

Blended unconsciousness
   Of drivel
    Is like drool and
      Empty words
        Holding tension, tissue
          Transfusions—
    Tensile and bonded
      By the sticky
     Sweet taste,
    False nectar
      Of Untruth.

1706

there is the decaying
   solar plexus
of self-absorption:
   black and spotted
     hinting at the ego's decomposition.

the ego
has a functional orbit,
the grasping trajectory will take
   you off course
   and hold
   you at bay—
so far out of reach
   as the heart
will be cold,
   really too icy
   to touch.

satellites
   will be thought
to be guideposts—
   because
you, the other,
   will be grounded
so fully into and on this earth.

where I reside
now
is always—

🌿 1707

The sun
  Is a dying star,
Speckled and folding
    In,
While the moon
  Is cratered
And so cold to
  The touch.
  There
Is no gravity
  And the breath
Is truly lifeless—
  Sucking out
And floating, a tetherless
  And timeless
  Archetype:
   All that
Will never settle
Into my orbit,
   As I am not suited for such—
   And the
   Fact that we
   Were suited
    Is really out of this
       World—

1708

To rekindle
 Is to touch the grace
 Of the wind
  Blowing through
 The fallen leaves—
  Dusting as it reveals
 Scattered starseeds:
  Emblems of the potential,
   Future's holdings,
  Not as bio-engineered monocrops,
  But diversity amongst
   What was meant to be
 Before the eclipse
  And the shooting stars
   Falling into
  The alone and barren land
With freighted galactic cargo
   Of despair,
    Separated from the Source.

Fading starlight
   Met with the warblers
    Before the migrations
   And the owls began thinking
   Of roosting for the day.
  A lumbering movement was delicate
    Rather than shifty
   As twilight bled into dawn.
  One did not meander off the path.

There is neither collapse
  Nor trespass
  Into other fields,
   As Source does not seek
  To ground and claim a new point—
   To make Ursa Minor

               The Asian tiger or
                    Trumpeted elephant.

Let go
     And bleed hope
                    Into the reborn
                    Of always.
          The trajectory
          Carries the certainty
          To tell the story
            That North is North,
               The star is overhead
          As it shoots
               Past like a bowed archer's
          Call to glory.

1709

What,
   What is the dark
Soft fold of sadness?
    Not knowing what's
     Finished and
      What's begun—

Sun sets and rises
    As constellations
Pasted into the deep
    Mystery are
   Lit by the source,
  Power,
    Unfolding light
   Stretched
     Between 2 palms,
    Pulled
     Towards the potential,
      The core of it
     All.

1710

6 days into space
   And
It's cold
   To the bone
     Cold
Pressure
Or lack of
     In this atmosphere
The perspective is too large
     And distant,
Definitely apart.

1711

The longest dark night
  Goes by halves and halves
  Never reaching the end
  Points of x, y, and z
  On only a 3-D graph
  Only by guessing
  Blinded and deafened
  By the silence of separation
From source
  Is profound when done
  Even if it was a breech birth
  Or emergency cesarean
  Still upside down
  Incubated after the exit
  From doctors misjudging
  The birthdate
  Or even promoting the premature
  Due to a holiday
  Like Flag Day which no one
  But the golfing obstetrician observed
  Having paid too much for the country
  Club and education loans.
Luckily no miscarriage
  Of justice, truth in its scarring
  As the deep majesty of riddled sky
  Is just too damn alone
  Without the umbilical cord
  To form the constellation
  As the placenta fell from the sky.
  And it's been a rocky ride since
  To say nothing
  And there are other things to hold
  The potential at bay
  And offer the trespass
  Of ungloved hands into and under
  While writhing with contractions

All in plain sight
Yet severity and spasms
Hidden by glory crowning
In its Truth.

1712

To surrender requires
    No need for dominance, coercion
    Nor contusions from the blinding
    Deceit of hypnotic mind control
    That blinds the eyes
    From a man
    With hands bound
    All behind the back.
Rather surrender is into
    An unfolding, one petal
    Unto the next
    Such that bouquets,
    Fertile fields of Absolute
    Loamy Truth
    May spring forth with a resilience
    Regardless of withholding droughts,
    Muddied and slurried intrusions
    From corrupted language of the heart,
    As the always to them
    Is discrete isolated moments
    Of greed for all the crops
    In plain sight
    When not blinded and gagged,
    Enslavement
    For the targeted.
The cosmic born from the aromatic bouquet of Truth
    Is neither derelict nor arbitrary
    Like rotten seeds thrown
    To the howling wind,
    As if only a howl could
    Keep one frozen and shuttered to the frosted ground.
Resilience is untamed wisdom
    Neither genetic anomaly nor cloning nor monocrops
    As a means to withstand the poisoned strain.
    It is having weathered and watched
    And touched the glory of grace

Such that one breath into the next,
These seeds, one generation into the next,
Will not rot or mold or decay
 In the face of graceless greed
 Held high in gated regions
 Oppressed by fear in all its glorious forms
 Such that love and light cannot be seen in Truth.
The patience of waiting so long
 Was the insistence not to bud nor seed and sprout
 In the face of the toothless wide-gapped and lecherous:
 Smiles from stolen truth and power
 From brainwashing all those
 Into drones, such that honey and nectar
 Could never truly form, nor pollination be
 Except by extraction and manipulation
 Like some mad scientist in his lab
 In his gated fallen paradise
Of jailed time with stolen identities, keys to treasure
And countries of the heart that once knew how to love,
Such that the symbiotic nature, and having no potency
Nor ability to make even the false honey
Requires the parasitic nature
And all the illusions:
Mildewed honeycomb edifices, parapets, and moats
Suffice as the true manna, the taste of one,
 As the pollinators evolved in the face
 Of the masked impotency.

1713

The Big Bang,
    Revised and corrupted,
    Lacks the golden expanse
Of the heart.
    Rather violation comes in,
    Never having touched and formed
Into galaxies.
    Radiation parts the heart
    Seed atom
In the palms.
    Aberrations of black holes
    Into and of the soul
Lack shadows—
    As greed swallows
    The sun
Distilled into a vacuum—
    Inside out
    And upside down.

1714

If the Dance Is in the Heart

If spring's dance is in the heart,
    What does winter's frost
      Hold still and true?

Blossomed like cherries
    Already fruited
    Sweet, succulent and pitted

From the stemmed branch
    Divided by the grace
    Of sun, stars, and moon

The eclipse has purpose to
    Fold into shadow
    Like the changing dialects

Into one region and country
    From another
    With historic boundaries

Based on geography, terrain, and severe
    Altitude, aligned with compass
    That is all so outdated

Now there is no timestamp
    For hours and wages
    Are not with stricture and debt

Wide-open sky of blended
    Truth of tongue
    To skin and breath

On the nape, the apex,
    The whisper
    Of knowing the boundary

Is never clinging to past
    Nor futuristic beyond
    Your touch

Which may be gone
    Tomorrow, today, this moment
    But it reaches and opens

To receive the next moment
    Of longing for a stretch
    Holding all as a continuum

To behold the ever-folding promise
    And knowing of love
    Neither possessed nor holding

But breathing as one wave into
    The next as it arcs with momentum
    Potential and exactitude

Of knowing it all will
    Be as it will
    So willingly

Be true and honest
    As the constellation blazes
    From the dark mystery

Of all
    And up close
    The flowered sepal

Allows the sweet wind
    Neither siroccan nor arctic
    To carry me afar

And begin anew again
    Always close to the origins
    As Truth is Truth

And seasoned love
    Is heart folding into scarring alone
    Healed together

So the forest of this love
    With species indigenous to the climate
    And orchids in the hot house

Seedlings sprouting with promise
    Dirt under the nails
    Only to rediscover

There is no barrier
    From one heart to the next
    Or star to star

Constellation to sun
    As the commonality of the Big Bang
    Is too much larger

Than being right towards wrong
    Left to right
    About church on Sunday

Or temple tomorrow
    Or the mosque at dawn
    Drums in the jungle

Of loving and knowing
    There can be no imposition
    Into our paths

To be on the journey
    Sacred and private
    Creation would never want

Competition, destruction, and vanity
    In the name of God or Gods
    Rather embracing the diversity

And commonality of the beautiful
    Landscape and you can be the artist
    In watercolors, and I can be

Molding clay, while this or that
    Sings love while they sweep the street
    Such that heart to heart

The planet can be released into
    Love and acceptance
    Of knowing the sequence

Is without hierarchy.

1715

An angle is such
   From all perspectives
   Yet severity flavors
   And tempers
   From the lack of sun
   Or shadows too tall and long
   Blown out of proportion
   Like a ticking bomb
   On tracks heading
   Into the horizon
   At the perpetual state of dusked truth
   From all the arid dryness
   And shock
   Of electrical forces ungrounded
   In this world
   That did not drop from innocence into evil
   As a straight shot
   Rather born into the naiveté
   The lesson has been to find the innocence
   After the asp swallowed it whole and unfruited
   As the garden was always held long and dark
   In this shadow
   Which finally just finally is fruiting in its Truth.

1716

I need to know
    By taste
  The sweetness, nectar
   Of this
     Heart of mine
       In your palms,
      And to me
        That translates to
        Knowing the tenderness and awe
        And trust that you will not
        Decimate nor destroy
        And manipulate as history
        Which precedes me—

I need to know
    There is no agenda,
    But to love and join,
    Celebrate who we are together and apart,
       And protect this golden jewel
       Of fragile vulnerability
       That still needs salve
       And healing from such blows.

I need to know
    That I may root
    Into your palm
    As the soil for our fertile love
      To fruit and seed
        And ripen in all
        The seasons as we
       Grow old and weathered
         From all the years
           Of watching sunsets on a
          Rock on a hill
           Tethered only
           By what we are
             Together and
            Apart.

1717

What's in the graced
    Touch of palm
        To this heart of truth?

What it is
    Is the remainder

Seemingly like long division
    In grade school,

And I'm still trying
    To grow up from these remnant numbers

To let the stalks and blossoms
    Reach up from the ages

For the inhalation
    Of deep sultry smells

Fragile spring's hope
    With summer's fruiting

And the seeding of the fall
    With the shadow's remainder

That never seems
    To reach the endpoint.

Like ½ into ½ into ½'s
    Teaching that the temporal "now" never is nor was

As that point
    Ceases to be

As it's truly all absolute.
    Yet, this grieving is like a long shadow

At high noon, too hot, blistering hot, and no respite,
    Before the draw

And it's the separation vs. Truth.
    I wonder if you see the shadow,

The fragility of this all held too long in the dark
    Of a hybrid seed

A genetic anomaly to me
    And yet of me

To withstand
    The blight, drought, and competition

Even though it was the desert
    Alone.

And yet, held so apart
    By this wandering grief

Like a beggar going corner to corner
    Looking

For deep radiant warmth
    And tenderness of tendrils.

Dear God,
    Can you please let me know

You see the radiance
    And allow me to be?

The grief of history
    Makes me stay apart

As your presence
    Brings hope and knowing

And much reflection
>   Of despair.

I think the sobbing may start
>   Before the dormancy has turned

Into spring
>   And the confusion of seasons

Going backwards
>   And you step forward

Without me
>   When you see how stained, fragile

And in need,
>   Like a famine

Of love and touch
>   And understanding and acceptance

As I have never seemingly had
>   That from a family

Other than my father,
>   A lament

And will you
>   Simply walk these tracks

Looking to destroy, to resent
>   And misunderstand and rationalize

Your hatred for me such that
>   The amplitude may break

Me forever into
>   A corral for the wild

Caged, such that
    I may never get out.

I am truly so scared of letting myself love
    And loving, of surrendering,

As the surrender has always
    Been me taken hostage

Or landing in a war, being the agent
    In the French Resistance,

And not as it should be—
    The surrender to heal

Together and apart.
    And I am just too much

To ever truly be received, loved, and known?
    The weeping is held back

Barely
    And sword to bed,

My arm is tired from wielding
    And yielding,

And generosity of heart is not
    Weakness of spirit.

Dear God,
    I am on my knees,

Falling, falling, falling,
    Yet, not into an abyss,

An endless free fall of darkness:
    Where I have been for decades,

A grief that will
    Never UNFOLD

    Into divinity's graceful embrace,
        The grounded surrender into the
            Absolute.

1718

Do you know
  That
 Alarms set me off?
  Delay means manipulation,
   Standing up for myself,
     As no one ever has,
    Means I am responsible for it all.
Shyness means rejection,
Misinterpretation means intentional neglect,
Caring always has a hidden meaning of untold calculation.

I am like the dead body
  Ripped apart by the vultures,
My ego
  Was eaten so long ago,
And the shadow
  Is this deep stain
  Tethered to memory
     Recall.

I think I've climbed Mt. Everest
    A million times, naked
    Blistered and raw
Trying to get as close
    As I can to something, anything
   Only to be
   Starting over like some mad nightmare
     Of men jumping out of the TV
     Chasing me to the threshold
     Only to start
       All over again and again
       Until woken in cold or hot sweat.

I learned how to deal with the terror
       Alone
         Breathing in and out

Always alone
Permanently alone.

1719

And in the voice
  Trebles divinity
  In its grace
  Reaching out
    With a magnified glory
      Of light, touch, and taste
    Healing hearts
      Through time and ages
So that we may emanate
      And awaken that love
      And gift in others
Such that this seemingly effortless grace
     Is arced back
     And grounded safely
      Into and always,
    As there never was giving away
      Of self at the deficit
      Of the heart,
  But replenishment of beauty
    Is the song sung
     At the dawning, arcing
      Into dusk
  So that sun, stars, and moon
     Which have always
  Danced in and around
    Know that the gravity
      Of the orbit
      Was not elliptical
But surrendering into the knowing
And holding truth
    Of love and being love
    As your own
    And that the
      Absolute of perfection
    Becomes evident as an illusion with no endpoints,
     As the cloak

Of the competition with self
Dissolves into the open heart
   Of divinity, grace, and truth
      Held in the awakening of one constellation
         After the next.

1720

What is the sign
   Language of love?
     Fertile, seeded, and to be
Even
In the face of a twisted torrent,
   Tongues forked
      Holding no truth,
Only the viper's
    Fanged greed
      Of deceit.

Toxic venom
    Veils a patina
    From here to there,
And in touching time
     Heart to heart can be divided
For the yield.

Seedlings bringing forth a resiliency—
As the crop was always
     In the distaste
      Of false tongue,
        Slithering and hissing
Taking the union of self to all
    And never knowing
      What to do
      At all
       With it
        Even—
Except never look at
    The self truly.

1721

Division into division
   Halves into wholes
   Divided by halves eternally
   Yields no endpoint—
    Nothing to be held
   In the lack of resolution.
  Hidden beneath and in
  The never-ending equation
   Is the mystery of negative numbers
Divided into negatives—
   There can only be
     Wholes,
   Positives.

1722

Beech leaves
   Arc over the crown
   Shading and swaying
Sorta dancing with the soul,
  Outlines no longer veil
  The softened shield.

  No longer armored,
Although vestiges, old emblems
  From countries long ago forfeited
    Not to dreams,
     But destiny of truth,
  Breathe in and out and not only dare,
    But sweetly enter
      The sacred holy ground
        Of ecstatic union
     Of earth, sky, and beloved self.

    In the moment now,
   Radiance of untold truth,
    But all known to you,
       Always like clouds
    Shifting into openness of
   Untethered touch to touch
     Of always being the oxygen
     To fill the soil, the soul.

1723

Division into dawn
   Is perhaps
   The darkest hour,
     Just before the husking dusk

   Hush, no hint,
      Not even a treble,
Faith in knowing it will
      Appear.

Color-coded
  Textures on my fingertips
  Taste like manna, sweet nectar
Of me
  As I am wedded again
  Into the grounded
  Beloved me
  With soft talc,
  Rose petal
Path of compassion
    Emblazoned with the hope
    That all may awaken
      To the grace
      Within the love
      That we
      All possess.
        In truth.

1725

Objectification is
   Attempting to dominate
 With external containment
 As if by such
     Countries, resources,
    Bounties and whores
    Are named and
    Could be lorded
    Like pirate booty or
    Stolen art treasures in
    WW2, as if anyone
    Truly owns any of it—
The creator is the artist.

And all the buying and selling
     Truly is the emulation, the
       Greed, to attempt to claim
      The other as their own
    Thru conflict, domination,
     And simply greed
     In all its self-deceit
       Rationale.

1726

In the calm of it all—
   There is neither eye of the storm
   Nor ferocity itself
    But sincerity of tenderness
     Of dappled wind
     Sensing.

Historic trauma
  Empties not into
    The hand of God
  But your inhale and exhale
    Is breathing life
      Back into
      The vicinity
        Of scars, old rusted
        Cars parked in violation
        Too long
          When the cops never
            Even ticketed
          Nor did one
            Notice the flat tires,
          But vandals
            Dented and banged
            Scraped graffiti
              Into heart
              And womb.

      Ripped and torn
          Membranes of what
          Was then rewritten as truth,
        Injuries too small and tight
            To even speak
      As the atom bomb
      Penetrated and ripped a small child's slumber:
          Every
      Holy war,
          Apocalypse, has been in that body,
        When there was no protection,
            But collusion of left and right,
        And the envy.

              Now that the combat
              Is over

Blame holds
> Like plastic band-aids,
> Over a gaping wound—
> Intentional denial of soul triage,
> Lesions may be covered
But they run so deep and cratered
Vacant and empty
> Lifeless and cold
> As the purpose
> Was to render one mute,
> As stories could not and would
> Not be told.

To remember and release
> Alone and the fear
> Of true masculinity
> Has been the misperception
> That passion is rage,
> And thus, it would
> All begin again
> Not as seasons
> Cycling into rebirth from decay,
But as that seizing terror
> Reigning
> From within the soul.

In between
> The step forward
> Is a stuttering pause:
The shame, humiliation, and doubt
Riddling me like bullets
> From the executioner's firing squad.

1728

A never expired star
    Has fallen from truth
    Into the palm of the fire,
And your constellation is held true
      As I learn the heart
      Was always safe
   In your palm outstretched,
      Whispering love
         Into
   The ecosystem
Parched too long,
     Evolution and genetics
       Of adaptation
Enabled me to exist without
      Knowing the feel and touch
      Of your love running
      To my tendrils
   Extending always
     Past
The full moon into the
     Always,
The only constellation
      That has been guiding and pulling
    Us together
      Again, always.

1729

The energy field of trust
   Is a current that
   Folds into and out
Of anything that is out of touch
    And one taste,
So, the true surrender into love
  Is knowing truth to truth
     Heart to heart
     Nectar into nectar
Is trusted truth,
    Always present,
    Reborn as the clouds
Parting to reveal the
Star pattern above and within the heart
That has always been
    Always obscured.

1730

In that fire,
   The heart is true surrender

     Unawares
  Awoken as dying
Embers,

  Ending the long winter,
Purified by the starry banks
    Of our constellation

    Of 1 into 1 into 1
   And we are

Awakened and known,

  In the complexity and simplicity
Of it all and receive

    As a gift

  You have waited
    Always knowing.

1731

Like the accordion,
   Strung out
    Before the pushing in,
As sound is released
   Hand to key.

1732

Faces strung out,
   And too many to know,
  To count,
    And you are neither
    Here nor there,
But in the heart,
     Beating,
   And that scares me
   Due to a whirlwind
      Of unknowing
   That couldn't possibly be
      Mine,
         Ever.

1733

Shadow
    Into shadow
    Boxing and unlaced
    Gloves
    Heavy hand swollen
     Bruised and sweaty
     Collection of grief
      And sodden
       With a gauzy
      Untruth.

1734

It's like being set up
    Again and again,
And truly,
    What is the grief?
Knowing the path has been shown,
   Tasted and touched,
    And yet, the recipient
    Never took the truth,
Unless stolen from the pocket,
      In full light
      For false crediting.
The sorrow
  Is knowing it's all your
  Creation, choice, and want
  To play the victimized
    And the jailed truth
  Will never set you free.

1735

Isolated and separated
  In a sea of voices
Does not translate to
    Faceless loneliness,
  As the power of aloneness
  Is knowing the heart breathes
      Truth.

1736

A rendering to the bone,
   Adrift in the rancid smoke
   From rekindling again and again
To leave a path—even a spark
   So I could be found.

A dislocation and disconnection
   To know
You will appear when the embers
Have become
     Charcoal
     To make a traceless point
     In this footed space.

1737

Is this all playing out as
  A witnessing such
 That it will never
  Manifest in actuality?
    Never, naught, and you will
      Run and run and run,
      Traceless, in place,
      And out of touch and taste.

1738

Perhaps
   It will appear
  Traceless
 And dreamy
    Like the moon
     Rippling on water's edge,
Tides blurring
    With tears,
And eclipses
    With full bellies
    And coffers.

1739

Everyone's here,
    And dancing amongst and within
      Is the question:
        What is it
          That I feel closed from?
The heart is damaged
      From all the deceit, lying,
      Addiction to self,
        And I know you are going far away.
      And yet, it hasn't been
      Without warning.

Grief
  Is the dark night
  Of seeing the hinting orb
     Of dawn wearily hoisting
           Over the hills and mountains
           With mists to bring the warming breath
  Thawing and gently rousing
  Truth and trust and faith.

Sweetness dribbles
        Into the crippled surrender,
   Healing arthritic immobility of the heart
         To know or to have known
         Being blinded by the warmth of the arcing sun—

         —As if this planet, me, was in the
         Far reaches of our solar system
         Pluto
            So well evolved, adapted, or just stuck in
            This dark terrain
               That does melt and transform
               Ice into gases
               As its odd angle approaches the sun.

In truth, without this Helios
          It would be too dark to know
          With eyes like ours,
    And so you are this radiance
          That has brought definition,
               Trajectory and transformation.

1741

The anxiety
  Is to surrender
  And what it all meant
     Before
    The atom bomb,
And to recall, really reclaim
    The known truth of peace:
  Each moment
    Is truly unknown,
       And this allows the exhale,
         Like one giant wave
           Cascading over me, you, us.

1742

If the heart
  Betrayed
The beat,
    Hidden by
The eclipse
      How would
        I know
          You?
          Truly, how?

1743

The surrender
    Is no longer
    One blind step
        Into mire
            Hidden by the quicksand
            Of possession.
Now it's a simple twist
    So complexly delicate
    As the tendrils of love
        Open in the breath
            Truth finally
        As the grieving releases long-held
            Positions requiring no emotional
            Opening nor vulnerability
        But seemingly asunder.

1744

If the painted sky
  Was held tight
  Like the canvas
    Stretched
  Horizon to horizon
  Zenith to nadir
    What would the palette
     Render?
The trust to see
  The beauty
Of textures now revealed
  As the sun
  Folds behind the hill
    And into your heart
Cupped between the
  Mountains
  Like my hands
    Seeing your truth.
And yet, the taste
  And smell of summer's potential
    Is evidently beyond
      The parameters of this frame,
    To be revealed,
      Perhaps, forever.

1745

The difference lies
   In being watched
    To dissect, disseminate
And allow the viewing
    As a means
    To define one's place
      With respect to all
        Else.

1746

What is freedom
   But simple acceptance
   Of circumstance
      Without active intrusion
       Of being consumed
         Like a plague
        By others,
A simple breathing in and out
        Such that
Tongue tip to palate roof
      Allows the
        Opening, as it were,
        And is always.

1747

If the constellation
  Were birthed
    From the palm to heart
Where is the evolution of maturity,
        Wisdom?
        Standing before these eyes,
          Truly from,
Breathing an inhale and exhale
        In mindfulness,
           Knowing that it was
           Always present, fertile
           And fruiting into me, you,
           Us, always.

1748

The trajectory was way
    Off in speed, force, and velocity.
And yet, the amplitude of knowing,
    Never ceased to be,
Hidden construct of
    True separation,
      As an illusion
    From source,
As a lesson in knowing,
    Love is always,
    And never left
      Behind like lost luggage
    In the space
      Shuttle into time and constellations
    Of heart and mind apart
    And now in union.

1749

If there was a chain
 To lock the fence,
You'd be in, sweetheart,
 Always in,
With key,
 Armed with my love,
And free to be
 Always.

1750

An isolated echo,
  And I solidly
Wonder why
    It's all occurred,
And the trespass
     Again and again,
 Now only witnessing
 The vulgarity, intrusions
 Of myopic vision
As I let go of the noose
    They apparently
    Hung all the deception by,
Dirty laundry,
    Stained and tainted
    Blowing vagrant
      Ungrounded
    Seedy off-color
      Seasoned
    Desiccation
      Back into the
      Origin, source
      Of the demarcation.

That tired,
   Like a long yawn,
Exiled from it all,
    Letting go of suspended
      Untruth,
    Belonging to the liar,
     Whom I believed again and again,
And acceptance is neither
Comparable nor equated
    With stealing bounty
    And desecration
      Of holy grounds.

1752

Speaking truth
   And the conveyance
   Leaves me wording and mouthing,
     "Why and how?"

   I am simply revisiting
    It all to let it
      Go beyond
   The vanishing point
     Such that no
     Trespass will and
     Shall occur again.

1753

Not being seen in truth,
    The distortion of it all,
  As big-bellied men,
      Come close
    And shielded for the
        Recourse,
    And know I don't
      Belong in a bar
        Collective any longer—
And realize the illusion of
      The tribe
Was simply to extract
      From me
        All.

1754

Textures and scents
    Of where it began,
And understanding
      Impotency
Is the inability to
        Follow thru
           Succinctly.

1755

The truth of injustice
   Finding currency
Inverted such that
     The equal exchange
Is void,
     And apparently
The one-way converter
      Leaches out
Giving false color and
     Saturation in vibrancy
Leaving an isolated
     Echo
Where it all began.

1756

Burrowed and alive
   There is breath
And wholly
      No division of time and thought,
     Only absence of touch,
        Taste and tenderness,
As the stalk
     Has rotted
     To the
        Earth.

1757

The collective
  Is not arbitrary,
But intentionality of self-interest,
    To pay the karmic debt
    Of insidious absorption
      Into false reality.
It is only truth bound to truth
    That allows true freedom,
    Purpose and speech,
Without the demand
    For things and trinkets
  Bound to the wrist
    Like objects
      Into clay,
        Unfired, and full of
          Air bubbles waiting
          For the explosion.

1758

Paranoia
   Stems from mistrust
  Like the stalk
    Bound into a false substrate
   Of neither soil nor earth
Complex of abandon
     From competition
     As a false emulation,
     Emulsified truth.

1759

Flashing sporadic
   Lights
And I'm grateful
   I don't have epilepsy
      In actuality.

1760

To be found, discovered
    By myself
Is like touching a crater
     Of the moon,
On the dark side,
       Perpetually
         Apart from warmth, touch, and love—
To be alone folded into
      Darkness always,
Such that narcissism
      From others
    Is always the cloak
        To knowing.

1761

Folded into an alone
    Space,
A vacuum lacks
    Gravity
Of purpose,
     Cold, so cold,
And this heart will stay
     Alone forever.

1762

Forever alone
   And hidden
From touch and feeling,
   The treasure lies so
   Buried that even
The oldest hound with
   The sharpest still legendary smell
Wouldn't dig up this bone,
    Even if starving and dying,
They'd rather walk
     Silently and slowly
    Limping into the woods
      To a
       Timely exit
From the false feminine.

1763

I wonder where
  And how
The youth, beauty, and innocence
Got siphoned
  Or hurled
Into outer space,
Such that galaxies
    Formed with the sole
    Intent
Of mirroring back
    The demise
   And the ugly face of it all,
Backhanded, branded
    Insult, false blame,
   Guilt, and such rancid
    Lack of truth.

1764

Why is there such
  A giving away,
    A focus of taking,
  With no recourse of action,
      But dancing
  In the false ecstasy
     Of thievery?

1765

All cycles run their
    Course,
  And yet the path
      Never ceases
    Until the still point
    Has been touched and
    Tasted as a
        Cycling season,
          Itself.
    It's not the intensity of speed
       Nor lack of,
  That cultivates implosion,
       Explosion, destruction,
But the vibrational shift,
    The unloading that
    Lets it all go.

1766

Long
  Hidden in plain
Sight
    Like the womb
    Folded over,
Before the magnificent
      Rebirth of Self from
        Self into Always.

1767

I am never going
  To be found,
Perpetually lost, adrift, at sea,
   And neutered and devoid
   Of any essence of truth,
     Trust and knowing—
   Hearth full of ashes
   From burning fires for you,
     Too long.

1768

Rambling voices
   Idle
 In the passing lane,
Construction signs, yields,
  And flashing lights
Go unnoticed
  As the empty space
  Is filled with longing,
    Manipulation,
  As a means to
   Find false truth,
    Always.

1769

Dedication to self
  Like an insecure prayer,
Or a counterfeit candle
  Lit in The Church,
  A false penny
    Paying the debt,
And the piggy bank's
  Been broken open
  Too many times
  To count
  The emptiness.

1770

Using
   Is not just for blatant
     Addicts,
  But everyone bound
     To subtle manipulation—
    It's a choice, A or B.

1771

Visible tears
  In a small town
  On a rainy day,
And no glasses to shield
  The sadness
From the sight of others.

In plain sight, unexplained
    View, with no
    Words, taste and
    Texture to share,
      Just the universal
      Knowing of tears in
        The eye,
          Dust, of course.

1772

Beautiful hair
    Of innocence,
Resilience of the heart
    Still held tightly
        By the tangled roots
        Of the familial tribe,
And false safety in knowing
    They will catch you,
        Allows the free flow
      Like a river
    Tumbling and cascading
Out of reach,
    And I know
That will never be me,
      Again.

1773

Safety lies
    With the pen to paper,
The heart reborn and released,
    Again in the form from
Symbol that has
    Universal meaning,
And ultimately individual
Interpretation.
    But the expression
Is the only place
    I have found
      True love,
    Nurturance
      From source into
        Soul.

1774

Perhaps,
  Pen to paper
  Is the legacy,
    All that was
      With father—
His entrusting, acknowledging
    And opening of it
Was the continuation
    Of knowing he is
      Always in the heart
Of union and dotted
    Into divinity,
But what has
    Been betrayed?
      And when?

1775

Translucent depth
    Sonic ranges
Of the core
  Of who I am,
      Now and always,
Of how could I
      Ever imagine
That I am
    Not enough?

1776

Exposed shoulder
    And beauty,
Sensuality, dripping
    Off, waiting
For your tongue
    To taste and lap
    It all up,
        Drop by drop,
        Ripeness and bounty
    Permeating down
        Your parched
           Throat.

1777

Trespass in plain sight,
    In feigned innocence,
Reeks of fouled
    Naiveté
To misunderstand
    The electric
        Danger
        You just
            Walked into,
Now sitting and
        Strapped,
Your karma
        Folds back to you,
Voltage by exponential
        Voltage,
And never a word
           Uttered.

1778

Stillness
Spills out
  In a shining
    Stunning
Moment that is
  My truth of always,
Only eclipsed by all
  The shimmering
Greed, feigned
    With fangs and
      A smile.

1779

Back against a board
   Of a barn
That's too old and derelict
   To even be
   Wrecked,
It's only good for tetanus,
    And Old Yeller
     Running rabid
    Around the truth,
Having swallowed all
   The lies in the
   Form, outline
   Of a viral
Implant of neglect, fear,
     Danger—
When in reality, it's all
   The karma
   Raped from
     My eyes and heart,
All under a smile,
     And never again.

1780

The sacred truth
   Is knowing not just,
  But also, being
    Irrelevantly not,
    Biased not,
  Being centered
    As it all twirls
     Around.

1781

To feel obligated
   To owe an
   Explanation
Is inherent with
   Giving the karma
   Away, bleeding it
    Dry
   Such that nary
  A heart seed
    Could ever bloom,
Plucked dry and withered,
   Rotten to the core,
   Your core—
    And your false seed
Is returned
    Without comment
    Nor explanation.

1782

I am so struck
  By the emptiness
    Of what's been said and
    Is said,
And the lack of meaning,
And this perpetually spun
  Narcissistic web
  To spin and prey
  As dictator
    Of this oh so small
World: your dictatorship
    Of self-aggrandized
      Ego.

1783

Patience runs too deep
    Like the septic
Wound hidden and
    Veiled in the
Cavity abscess
    Of waiting
For the shift of
    The self-oriented—
As if I was the
    Cause.

1784

The gloved, wonder of
   Truth, hidden
Behind the palette,
   Illusion of
     Heart to heart
     Bleeding out
        To form
        The masterpiece
        Of deceit.

1785

The love of it all
   Is unwinding
   Skin to skin
  And forming the
    Absolute from
  What the shadow
    Is not.

1786

Used goods
  Are like lost luggage,
    Banged from here
      To there,
    Busted open,
      Rifled through by
        Stale-smelling fingers
      Dripping
Stench, sweaty
    Disregard,
And finally arriving,
      Still declared
        As lost,
      1 day before the
          Insurance
  Kicks in,
      About 12 months too
        Late—
      And not even sharing
      The tales and
      Adventure
    As that's been
      Taken too.

1787

Why is this beauty
   Disregarded,
  Unmet,
   And misread
    As what it is not
     Rather than is?

Territoriality
  Like arbitrary
  Geographic lines
    Installed years ago
    From human footing—
    From the ant's perspective
      It doesn't matter,
      And from space,
        The colony isn't even
            Evident—
      And farther,
      The earth isn't
      Even a dot
        In my eye
          Or yours.
      But in theirs,
        It's part of their
          Blood.

1789

Bubbles in a puddle
    Coming and going
     Thru rain pouring
    Down,
And it's coming from
    Your heart
      Or mine
     Or together bleeding
     The wounds
      Dry, resilient,
        And healed.

1790

Is this winding path
  All leading
  To true resilience
  Of the known
    And union into and out,
And are we walking this
  Together or fully
  Apart?
Will it all get accessed
  Again and dissolve
  Into absolute
    Nothingness
    As voided
      Negation again?

1791

Resilience
  Upon the heart,
  Is it the essence
    Of Truth—?
    Truthful at times
Always like
  Day and night
With sweetness
  Like dawn and dusk
  Stellar nightlights
   Still in view
   And always
    In the palm of
      Your tender hand.

  Sacred
  Truth
    Created the dance
    For my eyes
     On my back
      In black sky
       Full mooned
       Love—
      Even in the
     New cycle holding
     All the hidden
    Destiny,
      Drifting through.

1792

I am so done
Filling in the blanks
   For others,
Putting in punctuation,
      Commas, quotes, dashes, and
         The period
So that the storyline
   May unfold.
I have stepped away,
    No longer tapping
    Out the letters
    And keying in
    The rescue,
      Happy, oh too,
    Patient ending.

1793

What does it feel like
    To know I've walked
      Away from holding
        Open the door,
          Bleeding the lifeline
          Through and into?
Have you figured out,
    You missed the
      Plane, train
        And even
    The rocket ship
    Of love,
Thrusters expired
    While they waited and wasted
      Fuel gone,
Dust-covered, historic
      Archaic remnant
      Of potential in 1 moment
Seen as
    Crude imagination
        Now.

1794

What's it like to miss me,
   And not being able to
      Step forward,
  Know the gap,
  Self-created,
  Never rendered truth?
What I do know
   Is what I see
And this sacred heart,
   This treasure,
Is in residence
   Finally of the ages,
And where it
     Safely and tenderly
     Should be.

1795

What is the mystery
    Of it all?
And where does the
    Insertion of faith, hope
      And trust
        Get tainted by
Uncertainty, greed, and
        Grabbing on too tightly?
And the denial
        When I point to the
       North Star
          And you tell me
          It was never there.
And the sadness
      At knowing
      The heart
        Was invited to be
          Held in your hand,
       And only because
        I know you can
         Do it so
         Sweetly
        And not suck the
         Pulp out
        After you macerate
         Our love
          With your shoe.

1796

I shifted
   Course
   A long time
   Undersea,
False constellations
    Navigating me
    Truly into
      The false heart, the
      Underworld,
So that I could have
The commonality
     To truly touch and
       Heal
      Within the eye
      Of the storm
     That always held the
      Stillness.

1797

Truth of navigation
    Allows the untold
    Story to unwind
Not like a long sultry
    Lift on a schooner,
Festooned with simple
    Love,
But hectic seas
    Parting for the
    Clear skies
        Painting the direction
        Of knowing and love
           In the heart.

1798

The fallacy
  Is friendship
  And the behavior
  Hidden behind
    Veils of receivership—

In reality, it's my cargo
  You want,
And the greedy palms
  Hold the fuse
That is blowing up
  In your face,
    Right now.

1799

Truth in navigation,
    Has no course,
    No boundaries
      Of hidden agendas
    Or scanning oceans
        For booty
    Or holding hostages
      For the telling.

The disappointment is seeing
    Who you are
      And waiting for the
        Reflection to
          Dawn on your
          Falsely innocent
          Face and
            To be reminded
        Never trespass into my
            Array with a posit of love.

17100

Resiliency
   Is returning to the fold,
   Knowing the certainty
      Threading from
         Moment to moment
           Is always
        The reception of divinity's
          Arm receiving
            As a constant
              Even with uncertainty.

17101

Finally uncovering
  The source
    Of betrayal,
    Tight-fisted
    And held in plain
      View
    Like a smoking gun to
     The temple
     Of one into all,
   And the path was never
  Earned but
  Taken like looted
    Treasures,
Under the false claim of
  Never using—

17102

Beyond the looted
   Lies the barren
   Grove
     Parched derelict
     Asunder
   And yonder
   As by choice
   It was never
   Grounded
Due to the idea
It should
All be given
Like purée
    Of false neglect
     And abandonment.

Ridden like a wild horse
   For too long
To believe the stories
   Of the bite,
As the old nag
   Lost its teeth
   And hold
Centuries ago,
    Not from old age,
    But the despot
   Pulling them out
   1 by 1
   Pliers
   And with their toes,
Eating grapes
   And basking
    In all the given
     And deceived
      Bounty.

17103

It is strangely challenging
   Not to thwack
      The novice,
When you see them
      Cheating in plain
      View, thinking
      The true mystic who knows
      Doesn't see
         All too well
         In the dark,
Even blindfolded
   I could smell
   This a million miles
      From my home and heart,
   Where you shall remain
      In barren exile
         From this fertile land.

17104

Fertile land
   Will not hold
     The fallen by choice
       Any longer.

17105

Circumnavigating
    The Globe
    On foot
      Is one thing,
But doing the axis
    Alone
      Is the only way
      To reach resiliency
        Of solitude,
        Of point of Truth,
          In constancy.

And with deep gratitude

Other poetry titles by Wendy E. Slater:

Full Circle Undivided, Poems-Volume 1

Into the Hearth, Poems-Volume 14

Of the Flame, Poems-Volume 15

The Ocher of Abundance, Poems-Volume 16

Visit Wendy E. Slater's website
www.traduka.com

www.ingramcontent.com/pod-product-compliance
Lightning Source LLC
Chambersburg PA
CBHW081430070526
44586CB00020B/2539